CRYPTO CURRENCY:

Introduction

The idea of cryptocurrencies is relatively a new idea. Just a few years ago, it was an idea that no one thought would ever become a reality. Who would think that you could have a whole currency available online, one that you are not even able to get paper versions of, and that didn't have a central authority control them? Today, there are many cryptocurrencies available, with the most notable being options like Bitcoin and Ethereum. While many people have heard about these various cryptocurrencies and some may even use cryptocurrencies on a daily basis, understanding how these currencies work is not that well-known. Most don't understand how these currencies started, how they work, and what technology is behind them to ensure that they will be trustworthy and work the way that people want them to. So, let's take a look at these digital currencies and what they are all about.

To start, a cryptocurrency is going to be a medium that you can use for exchange, just like what you will find with traditional currencies. The big difference that you will notice is that these cryptocurrencies are designed to exchange information digitally through the blockchain. This means that you will be able to use these cryptocurrencies just like you can with your traditional currencies, but all of the transactions will be completed online, rather than with the paper currencies that you would use at the store.

There are quite a few currencies that are available for you to choose from. The first cryptocurrency was Bitcoin, and it was developed in 2009. Once Bitcoin started to gain popularity throughout the world, many more cryptocurrencies, which are now known as Altcoins, became available. Some work similar to Bitcoin, but there are a few that were designed for slightly different uses.

Cryptocurrency is going to happen completely online. You will not be able to print off the coins or convert them into paper money to use. This is because when the cryptocurrencies are used, either to send money or to finish another transaction, it is going to be converted into lines of code that have a monetary value. This is why cryptocurrencies are often going to be known as digital currencies.

In addition to being able to use these currencies online, another benefit of using cryptocurrencies is that there isn't a central authority that is controlling them. With the economic issues of 2008, many people throughout the world stopped trusting government control over their money and were excited that cryptocurrencies provided them a way to have a trustworthy source of money without having any government interaction.

The reason that cryptocurrencies can be so effective without having to rely on the government is that of the innovative blockchain technology. We will discuss this technology more later on, but this technology has been able to change the face of many industries because it can process transactions instantly, is safe and secure, and the transactions that are placed on it can't be changed when they are done.

With many cryptocurrencies have been designed so that they decrease in production over time, which ensures that there will be a market cap with them. This is much different from traditional currencies because, with traditional currencies, it is possible for the government and other financial institutions to create more of the currency. This is how inflation occurs. On the other hand, the popular digital currency Bitcoin will never have over 21 million coins available to use. Not all of the coins are available in circulation right now, but the total amount will never get above this number.

While there are many different types of digital currencies that you can pick from, they are all going to be derived out of one of two protocols. These two protocols are known as proof-of-stake or proof-of-work. All of the digital currencies will be maintained by miners, who are basically people who have set up their computers and other machines who will participate in validating and processing all of the transactions that occur for a particular currency.

The history of cryptocurrency

Cryptocurrency came around at the perfect time for it to be successful. It would have had a lot more trouble gaining life and doing well if it had come about at any other time in history. Bitcoin was the first digital currency in existence, and it was first created in 2009. It is unknown who was the one to develop Bitcoin, but they go under the name of Satoshi Nakamoto.

Many people liked the idea of Bitcoin because they were tired of the economic failure that was occurring throughout the world at the time and they liked the security and freedom from government that they got when using these digital currencies. While it still took some time for Bitcoin to take off, it has reached big heights in recent times, with one Bitcoin being worth more than $11,400 right now.

The first altcoin, known as Namecoin, started in April 2011. This was created to form a decentralized DNS, which made it more difficult to censor the internet.

Then in October of 2011, Litecoin was released. Litecoin became the first digital currency that uses a scrypt as the hash function rather than relying on SHA-256 like Bitcoin did. This made it easier for the general public to mine these coins without having to get the specialized technology and machine that were required for Bitcoin. As these major players started to gain more traction in recent years and more people throughout the world started to join the networks. There are literally hundreds of digital currencies that are available online now, and you can choose the one that is going to meet your needs the best.

The market capitalization of digital currencies

Right now, Bitcoin is considered one of the largest digital currencies in market acceptance, notoriety, volume, and capitalization. However, it is not considered the most valuable of the coins right now. But since it is one of the most well-known currencies and it was one of the first, it is often seen as the most important. After Bitcoin, Litecoin and then Ripple are seen as the biggest names in digital currencies.

Another option that you may have heard about, known as Dogecoin, is an interesting one when it comes to market capitalization. This digital currency is often third place in terms of trading volume, but the market cap is going to be lower. This one usually ranks as number six.

The security of digital currencies

Since there isn't a government agency or a financial institution that is running these digital currencies, many people who are considering joining the networks may be a little bit worried about how secure their transactions would be on them. The security that comes with digital currencies is going to be two parts. The first part comes because there is some difficulty with finding hash set intersections, something that the miners will work on.

The second part is what is known as the 51 percent attack. This means that for any changes to be made in the network, for any of the transactions to be changed, the hacker needs to be able to gain control over 51 percent or more of the computers on the network. Since the users of these currencies are available all throughout the world, this is almost impossible to occur. This helps to keep the network as safe as possible.

In addition, these digital currencies are going to be less susceptible to being seized by the government, having issues with law enforcement, or having holds placed on the transactions like other things may. The transactions are instant and permanent, so you won't have to worry about missing out on payments or having to wait around. And with the help of the blockchain, you will be able to remain anonymous on these networks, making it harder for people to figure out what transactions you are completing.

These digital currencies are proving to have more security compared to traditional forms of payments and even compared to some of the big-name stores that we like to use. These big financial institutions and stores have run into a lot of trouble, with hackers always aiming to get on their databases and take the information that is there. It is all too common to turn on the news and hear that information has been compromised yet again. This means a lot of time and hassle on the part of the customer, and it can seem frustrating and like the company isn't doing anything about it.

There are some better security measures in place with these digital currencies. The blockchain is really an amazing feat of technology that not only helps to get transactions done in no time, but it is designed to keep your information safe. If someone goes onto the blockchain and starts to mess around, anyone on the network will be able to notice because the blockchain becomes a mess. It is almost impossible for the hacker to get ahold of your information and steal your identity. With that being said, you still have to take some precautions with your coins. While the blockchain may be pretty secure, there are still hackers who will want to get onto the network and take your coins right out of your wallet. You have to be the one to be vigilant about this issue; there really aren't any safety features in place to help with this. If your coins disappear because a hacker got into your account or because of a computer glitch, there is no one on these networks who will be there to help; the coins will just be gone. We will spend some time looking at the various backup options that you can use, such as hardware backup and cold storage, that will ensure your coins stay safe, even if something happens to them in your wallet.

Dealing with legality and taxes with cryptocurrencies

Another issue that you may need to deal with is whether these digital currencies are considered legal in your country. Most countries allow these digital currencies, with Vietnam and Iceland being the exception. In addition, China has already banned their financial institutions from working with Bitcoins, and Russia has said that it is illegal to purchase goods in the country with currencies that are not the Russian rubles.

While these digital currencies are allowed in your country, you may have to deal with the issues of taxes. This is seen in the United States where the IRS has already ruled that Bitcoin should be treated just like property when it comes to tax season. This means that any of the Bitcoin that you have can be subject to capital gains tax. This has put some restrictions on Bitcoin and the other digital currencies, and you have to be careful when reporting them on your tax return each year.

In the United States, you also have to be careful about other law enforcement. The United States has not prevented digital currencies yet, but they are making it more difficult to use. One of the main benefits of using digital currencies is that you can remain anonymous on these networks, making it harder for others to track your transactions. However, the United States government is setting up laws that would make it a requirement for the digital currency exchange sites to report information of all users, which would take away some of this anonymity that you are looking for.

It is important that you understand the laws for digital currencies in your country of residence. Technically anyone can get on a digital currency and use it, no matter where they are located throughout the world. However, if there are specific rules that prevent this in your country of origin, it is not a good idea to try and use the currency.

The best thing that you can do is take a look at some of the rules for your country of use before getting started. Most countries are fine with you using these currencies so that will not be an issue, but some do have limitations. In addition, you need to make sure that you understand the tax implications of using these coins, especially if you are making a profit from investing them. As long as you follow the rules in your own country though, you should be fine.

Services available with cryptocurrencies

There are actually quite a few services that you can use when you want to monitor various cryptocurrencies. This can be useful for the person who is interested in mining with digital currencies and who wants to fully do their research ahead of time. CoinMarketcap can be a good one to start with because this will allow you to see information about digital currencies including their market cap, the price, and the available volume and supply. Reddit is a good way to follow the trends that are going on, and CryptoCoinCharts will have a lot of information about the exchange rates of the different coins you want to work with.

Liteshack is another one to consider because it will allow you to view the hash rate for a variety of coins using the six different hashing algorithms. This site even provides you with a graph of these hash rates, which can help you to check on the trends that go with the coins you want to work with. This will make it easier to see if the coin is gaining in popularity or if they seem t be losing interest before you invest.

If you want to get into mining with coins (which can be very profitable if you learn how to make it work), then you need to use the website CoinWarz. This site will help you to look at the hash rate to determine which coin is going to provide you with the most profit. Mining can be difficult so figuring out where you will get the most money can help save you time and will make this endeavor more profitable.

There is a lot of potentials that comes with using cryptocurrencies, whether you want to use them for your own investing, you want to use them to make purchases, or you just want to learn a bit more about them. This is a new world that is still expanding, and there are a lot of great possibilities that are sure to come out of these digital currencies in the future.

Chapter 2 Choosing a Cryptocurrency

There are many different types of cryptocurrencies that have sprung about since the release of Bitcoin in 2009. As a result, there has been a wide amount of speculation as to which currency is the best to invest in and where you should be putting your attention. Many of these coins are viable competitors to Bitcoin, with some even being considered better or more advanced in their abilities and potential. Others seem to exist on a much smaller scale and may or may not provide the same value or benefits those larger coins might.

When you get started in investing in cryptocurrency, you want to make sure that you are investing in the right currency. You want to make sure that you pick one that is going to suit what you are looking for in regard to investment purposes, as well as one that you can rely on and ideally earn a profit from if you are in the business of trading.

To help you learn more about each coin that is presently available, where it currently sits in the marketplace, and why you might consider investing in it, we are going to explore the most popular and well-known coins that have become available in the cryptocurrency market.

Bitcoin

Topping our list of currencies is Bitcoin. This coin is the most popular coin because of how famous it has become because of being a pioneer in the modern cryptocurrency world. It was the first to launch, and it has topped the charts ever since. Despite other coins coming out, Bitcoin has remained at the top of the popularity ranking since its launch in 2009. Despite its popularity, however, there are other cryptocurrencies that are rapidly encroaching on its territory in the way of them being valid competitors in the marketplace. Bitcoin is said to be like a digital version of gold. It has been used globally for payment methods, and many different online and even offline merchants have begun accepting this currency as a form of payment for goods and services. When people discuss cryptocurrencies, Bitcoins are typically the first thing that comes to mind. These coins began at a value of $0 and were originally launched as a beta program. Developers wanted to try and see if they could find a valid cryptocurrency format that would work, and it's safe to say that they did. Not only is Bitcoin still in existence today and rapidly growing in popularity, with it rapidly approaching $13,000 USD in value, but also holds the title as the pioneer for modern cryptocurrency technology. It is safe to say that they certainly mastered the algorithm and successfully designed a cryptocurrency that is valid and useful when they launched Bitcoin!

Ethereum

Since its launch in 2015, Ethereum has rapidly become second-in-place for the best cryptocurrency to get involved in. Despite being second in the cryptocurrency hierarchy, however, Ethereum has an incredible addition that Bitcoin does not have. That is, Ethereum has been designed to not only perform basic transactions but also to perform complex contracts and programs. It does so by using the Blockchain technology that was introduced upon the creation of Bitcoin.

Ethereum smart contracts and programs are essentially complex contracts that are created to determine how and when money will be issued. Once certain conditions are met, money will be released to the appropriate party. If, however, these conditions are never met, the money is never released.

The interesting thing about Ethereum is that it is actually created to be more of a family or set of cryptocurrencies versus a single cryptocurrency like Bitcoin. This means that Ethereum hosts several "tokens" which are used as a currency form. Some include DigixDAO and Augur. These tokens are then used to complete payments and transfer funds. Each unique token carries a different value. It is quite similar to how you may carry coins in your own physical wallet. Some might be worth just $0.10 whereas others are worth $1 or $2. When you invest in Ethereum, it pays to invest in several different tokens to further diversify your portfolio and maximize your potential gains.

Ripple

It is important that we talk about Ripple despite it being considered one of the least popular cryptocurrencies on the market. You do not want to get involved with something without fully understanding it, and since Ripple is widely talked about, it is important that you are completely aware of what you are getting into if you begin exploring Ripple as a cryptocurrency investment option.

Ripple is a form of cryptocurrency that is less than a currency format and more of a debt format. The native cryptocurrency for this program is XRP, and it is not actually used as a medium to store and exchange value. Instead, it is used as a token to protect the network itself against spam.

Most people consider Ripple to be a poor investment and do not think it will last long or be worth it in the long run. Many cryptocurrency buffs call it a premined software and believe it is not a real cryptocurrency but rather a network. However, the banks appear to really like Ripple and have begun adopting the system at an increasing pace.

Litecoin

Whereas Bitcoin is considered to be digital gold in the cryptocurrency world, Litecoin is considered to be digital silver. This coin quickly launched just after Bitcoin, making it the second cryptocurrency to truly emerge on the scene of modern cryptocurrencies.

When they developed Litecoin, it is believed that they developed it as a "2.0" version of Bitcoin. They made it so that the transactions and mining process are faster than in Bitcoin technology, and also so that there are more tokens, as well as new mining algorithms.

This cryptocurrency was perfectly designed to be the smaller and more readily available version of Bitcoin. Whereas Bitcoin may hold higher marketplace value and popularity, Litecoin tends to be much easier for people to get started with and use in investments and trading.

The biggest setback with Litecoin is that people preferred to use Bitcoin over Litecoin and therefore no one ever found a real use for it. For that reason, people stopped using it widely and instead favored Bitcoin. However, the coin is still mined and traded, and many people hoard it just in case Bitcoin ever fails.

Monero

After Bitcoin was created, developers realized there were further ways that security could be enhanced and the algorithms could be stronger. As a result, they developed the CryptoNight algorithm and launched Monero. The biggest example of how these two differ is with the blockchain transactions. Bitcoin is hashed on the blockchain, and a trail of transactions follows it, always. There is no way to cut through this. With Monero, however, you can cut through them.

The first time that the CryptoNight algorithm was introduced was in a coin known as Bytecoin, and it was highly rejected by the cryptocurrency community. This was because the cryptocurrency was heavily premined. However, they managed to later launch Monero which is the first time they ever launched the CryptoNight algorithm as a non-premined clone of the original Bytecoin. Although many others have since emerged, Monero has maintained its position as the most popular variation of a cryptocurrency existing with CryptoNight algorithms.

Monero has continued to steadily increase in pricing, however the ways it can be used remains extremely small. For that reason, it may be worth investing in, but many people are losing faith that it will have any form of significant future in the economy or marketplace. Rather than being a good investment as a currency itself, the technology is a better investment as it provides a form of playground for the developers to build on.

Making an Investment Choice

Choosing which coin to invest in really depends on what you are looking for. If you want to have a basic coin that you can invest in and trade, Bitcoin is likely the best way for you to go. This cryptocurrency revolves around a single form of token and is the most popular, which is likely the very reason why the price has continued to steadily increase for nearly a decade since the technology was launched.

The next best form of currency to get into is Ethereum. This currency is rapidly sidling up to Bitcoin as the best cryptocurrency technology and easily takes second place as most popular. While Ethereum is more of a family of tokens versus a single kind, it is still a great cryptocurrency to invest in. If you choose to invest in Ethereum, make sure you choose one of the more popular token to invest in, such as the DigixDAO or Augur. Do your research before investing in any particular token so that you are not investing in something that will not earn you a strong return.

If you want to consider a less-expensive and still fairly valuable coin to invest in, Litecoin is a great place to start. While you will not make nearly as much return as you will with Bitcoin or Ethereum, it is a much lower buy-in and can be a great way to diversify your cryptocurrency investment profile and also protect yourself should Bitcoin ever fail.

If you are considering investing in something different that is considered to be more of a playground or a test program, Monero may be the way to go. While you likely will not get a strong return on this coin, you will be on the trail of a new form of an algorithm that has emerged in the cryptocurrency world. This means that if anything ever changes and goes strongly in Monero's favor, you will already be on board.

Avoid investing in Ripple at all costs. There is very little to be said about this program other than the fact that it is not widely accepted, not an advancement on technology, and will likely not go anywhere. You will not make a strong return on your investment and will likely find yourself out a lot of money if you trail this cryptocurrency and try to earn any form of return on it.

Making the Choice for Purchasing

If you are looking to get into a currency that you can both invest in and purchase products with, Bitcoin and Ethereum remain the two best choices. Both of these have a wide and ever-growing range of uses and are being accepted by more and more merchants all of the time. Not only are you likely to make a great return on your investment, but you can also actively use them for shopping and transactions to get an idea of what purchasing things with cryptocurrency is truly like. The other forms of cryptocurrency have a very small backing in the marketplace which means that there are few things you can actually purchase with them. While they may be okay for trading and investing, or diversifying your investments portfolio, they are not ideal when it comes to shopping of any sort.

Chapter 3 Uses of Cryptocurrency

Cryptocurrency is not just found in a small niche online that only a few people are able to use. In fact, the technology that helps run these online currencies is so innovative, that it is starting to take over many other areas of our financial world. This chapter is going to take some time to look at the various uses of cryptocurrency and how it is changing the way we do business in everyday life.

Ecommerce, Business and Local Merchants

There are so many ways that cryptocurrencies can be used and the reasons just keep growing. In fact, people have begun to invest in blockchain technology because this is the part of cryptocurrencies that will have the biggest impact on our financial futures and the way that we conduct business in the future. But even today, there are some big uses for cryptocurrency and it is already shaping the way that businesses behave.

Ecommerce

Ecommerce is probably going to see the biggest change when it comes to cryptocurrency. Currently, when we want to shop online, we have to visit the store that we want to shop with, pick out the products we want to use, and then provide them with a lot of personal information, including our names, addresses, and our credit card information just to get the product.

This information is then stored inside the merchant's system, and as we have seen over the years with a wide variety of data breaches, this information is not necessarily the safest when it is stored in this way. Hackers are more than happy to get onto whatever system the store is using and take all your personal information to use for themselves. This is not really an efficient way to shop and has limited the trust that people have for many companies.

Things are a little different with cryptocurrency. It is possible to shop online and keep your information safe. Blockchain networks are designed to help keep all the information safe and with the help of the miners, these transactions are coded and stored in an extremely secure manner. No longer do you need to worry about your personal information just sitting there for someone to take thanks to this great technology.

In the future, it is likely that more ecommerce sites are going to start implementing blockchain technology. This will allow them to build up more trust with their customers and can make it safer to use their websites without as much risk of hackers getting on. There are not many companies who have this technology right now, but it is likely to continue growing in the future. Just another way that the world of cryptocurrency is going to change so many aspects of the way we do business in the future.

Business

The world of finance and business are going to change quickly once they start to modify and use the blockchain technology. Many of them are still in the past, using a ledger and accounting systems that just don't work that well for them or for the customer. These ledgers have a few problems. The first one is that they are slow; it takes a few days for the transactions to go through and this really slows down the buying and selling process. This can be frustrating to a lot of people who may do online purchases. We are used to the world where things should be instant, but instead, they are still considered slow.

Another issue is that these ledgers are not that secure. Our information is present on these ledgers and all someone needs to do is access the system to see it. They will see your credit card information, your name, and even address and more for each transaction. The blockchain technology that is currently applied to cryptocurrencies is able to hide your information, while still making it transparent so that the transactions you use won't automatically be linked back to you.

Big banks often lose millions of dollars each year because of accounting errors and inefficiencies. The blockchain technology, if it is used properly, could solve some of these issues and make it easier for banks to lower their fees associated with errors and administration.

The good news is that there are already many developers who are working on blockchain platforms that can work for a variety of financial institutions. There are even some financial institutions who have already adopted these platforms in order to save themselves money and to provide better customer service overall. While the current technology may be too expensive or not the right fit for a lot of companies right now, it is sure to develop in the future.

Local Merchants

There are many local merchants who choose to work with these cryptocurrencies. Some are small enough that they will offer their products and services exclusively on the network of their choice (often Bitcoin right now since that is the most popular), for customers to use. Others will add this in as a new payment method. For example, they may accept cash, PayPal, and credit card and then they add on Bitcoin or another cryptocurrency for their customers.

Some of the bigger chain stores are choosing to join the cryptocurrency market as well, making it easier to use your coins at more places. Some stores still aren't accepting these kinds of coins, but you can use your coins to purchase gift cards to those stores, so there is an indirect way to use these coins and shop where you would like.

Trading and Investing

Many people are choosing to use cryptocurrency as a way to make money, rather than just as a way to make purchases without the hassles of big banks and government agencies. Investing is a great option with these currencies, especially since they are so new, and many people who take their time and do research find that it is a great way to make money while these currencies grow.

There are quite a few investment options that are available, and we will talk about these in more detail later on. Some people choose to buy stock in the cryptocurrency company and then earn dividends on that each year. You can find a company to invest in that is on the network (which works really well with Ethereum), or they can do forex trading and purchase coins today and then exchange it out when it is worth more in the future.

Since cryptocurrencies are so new, it is likely that even more investment opportunities are going to arise in the future. People are always looking for a way to make money and as these cryptocurrencies expand to other parts of the world and more people learn about them, it is likely that there will be quite a bit of money allocated and invested in cryptocurrencies.

Chapter 4 Benefits Of Cryptocurrency

The simplicity of cryptocurrencies is its main strength. The elimination of middlemen and other regulatory authorities along with the ease of transactions make cryptocurrencies a great option. In the initial phase, it might have seemed scary just like credit cards did during their initial days. You probably will have heard of different cryptocurrencies like Bitcoins or Ether. These cryptocurrencies make use of the ingenious blockchain technology that makes them secure. In this chapter, let us take a look at all the different advantages this currency offers to its users.

No scams

Cryptocurrencies cannot be forged because of their digitized nature. Not just that but cryptocurrencies eliminate the scope of a transaction being arbitrarily reversed by a sender. Credit cards create the possibility of a chargeback, and this is done away with this digitized currency.

Instant settlements

If you want to purchase real property, then regardless of whether you like it or not, there will be a few third parties like lawyers, notaries or brokers involved in it along with delays and fee payment. Cryptocurrencies are similar to a large database of property rights. The cryptocurrency contracts are designed in a manner that eliminates the involvement of third parties, and they can be enforced without the approval or third parties and any reference to other external facts. The time taken for the settlement of a cryptocurrency contract is far less than that required for a regular contract or agreement.

Lower fees

No transaction fee is payable on cryptocurrency exchange since all the miners are compensated for by the network itself. Even though there isn't a transaction fee, most users make use of third-party services for the creation and the maintenance of their cryptocurrency wallets.

Identity theft

Whenever you give a vendor or a merchant your credit card, you are automatically giving them access to your credit line regardless of the amount involved in the transaction. Credit cards function on a pull basis-as soon as the vendor has initiated a payment; the concerned amount is automatically pulled from your account. All cryptocurrencies make use of a push mechanism. The holder of the cryptocurrency needs to send the exact amount to the merchant, and only the holder can authorize such a transaction.

Ease of access

More than 2.2 billion people all over the globe have access to the Internet and smartphone, but not everyone has access to the traditional exchanges. Cryptocurrency is best suited for such people, and there are plenty of mobile-based services that help in the transfer of cryptocurrencies.

Decentralization

A vast network of computers spread all over the world make use of the blockchain technology for transacting in cryptocurrencies and maintenance of a database of transactions. A single regulatory authority like the government or central banks doesn't control cryptocurrency. It forms a collaborating power instead of a controlling one.

Universal recognition

A huge network of computers all over the world makes use of Blockchain technology for managing the Bitcoin database and the transactions. A network manages Bitcoin, and a single authority does not control it. Decentralization in here would signify that the system will operate on a peer-to-peer basis or a user-to-user basis. This helps to form a collaborative space instead of a controlling authority.

Universal recognition

There are no interest or exchange rates that control cryptocurrencies, and there are no transaction costs or charges levied on them. So, a user can make international transactions without incurring any additional charges. This saves time, effort and money while conducting a transaction. There is no system of electronic cash that you can make use of which isn't owned by a third party. For instance, in the case of PayPal, if the company is of the opinion that a particular account is being misused then they have the power to freeze all activity and the account itself without consulting the user. When you make use of cryptocurrency, you are the only one with access. Only a user with a private key can access his or her account, and no one else can do that.
When made use of in the proper manner, the potential of cryptocurrency is unparalleled, and no other currency can compete with it.

Chapter 5 How To Buy Cryptocurrency

There are two different ways to purchase cryptocurrency, the first is to utilize fiat cash (USD, EUR, GBP and so forth) to buy cryptographic money through a trade. These trades work a similar path as customary unfamiliar money trades do. The Costs change consistently, and like customary cash trade markets - they are open day in and day out. These trades bring in their cash from taking a little charge for every exchange.

Some charge the two purchasers and venders, some solitary charges an expense for purchasing. For security reasons, most of these trades will expect you to confirm your ID prior to permitting you to buy cryptocurrency. It is additionally imperative to take note of the sort of installments each trade upholds. A few takes into account charge/Visa installments though other just acknowledge PayPal or bank wire moves. The following are the three greatest and respectable money trades for buying Bitcoin, Ethereum and other altcoins with fiat money like US dollars, Euros or British Pounds.

Coinbase

Presently, biggest cryptocurrency marketplace on the planet, Coinbase permits clients to purchase, sell and store digital money. Coinbase is without a doubt the most novice agreeable trade for anybody hoping to engage in the cryptographic money market. When your ID is verified, you can purchase digital currency inside Coinbase in minutes, utilizing a bank account or debit card. Coinbase exchanges many cryptocurrencies including Bitcoin, Ethereum and Litecoin, utilizing fiat cash as a base.

Coinbase also has a completely working iPhone and Android application for purchasing and selling in a hurry, extremely convenient and easy. On the off chance that you pursue Coinbase utilizing this connection, you will get $10 worth of free Bitcoin after your first acquisition of more than $100 worth of Cryptocurrency.

Kraken

Situated in Canada, and popular for purchases in Euros, Kraken has the upside of more coin uphold (they additionally permit the acquisition of Monero, Ethereum Classic and Dogecoin) than Coinbase.

For other cryptocurrencies, for example, Dash and Golem, you will require admittance to a trade that encourages digital currency to cryptographic money exchanging.

Chapter 6 The Cryptocurrency Trade

What is cryptocurrency trading?

Cryptocurrency trading is pretty much like trading shares where you speculate cryptocurrency price movements. For this, a Contract for Difference (CFD) trading platform is used. The CFD allows you to speculate rising and falling prices of various global markets including that of cryptocurrencies. You can evaluate any cryptocurrency of your choice without taking ownership of those coins. In doing so, this allows you to choose your next actions carefully. You can either decide to buy if you think a cryptocurrency is about to rise (go long) or you can decide to sell your currency if you think its value is going to drop (go short).

However, to get access to all of the data about these underlying markets, you need to get full exposure and must first submit a deposit, also known as margin. Normally your profit and loss are gauged according to your position however by leveraging, or paying a margin, you can magnify your profits and losses.

You can also trade cryptocurrency through an exchange. This also comes with its own learning curve and gives you access to useful information. To do this, you need to have an exchange account, add the value of your assets and store your currency in your wallet before you can sell it in the exchange. In order to buy through an exchange, you must be buying the actual coins for yourself.

How do cryptocurrency markets work?

As we now know, cryptocurrency is a decentralized form of currency and hence the market is also decentralized. This means there is no central authority or a formal body like a bank or a government that is monitoring or influencing the market flow. The market relies on the internet and computers which have enabled it to become a global market. The exchanges allow the market to be monitored to a certain extent i.e. they allow cryptocurrencies to be bought and sold through an exchange and to also be stored in wallets. Since cryptocurrency is unlike tangible currencies that we use in our day to day transactions, its movements must be recorded in order for it to exist digitally. For this reason, we have blockchain, which acts like a book ledger and records all the movements of the cryptocurrency, meaning, for all transactions. If I want to sell my cryptocurrency to someone, I do so by using my cryptocurrency wallet. However, that transaction will not be final unless it has been verified and added to the blockchain. To add a transaction to the blockchain it has to be mined by crypto miners who are responsible for verifying and recording the transaction and they may also get a reward of cryptocurrency for mining it successfully.

What are the secrets of cryptocurrency trading?

To be a cryptocurrency trader requires guts, patience, and resilience as this process can be very stressful, as your precious investments are being put on the line. However, there are steps you can take as a trader to ensure that you are on top of your game. Here are some simple and practical secrets from successful crypto traders:

1. Be prepared

Having a clear plan and to being prepared is key to your crypto success. You must set a benchmark for yourself, as to how you will react when the market shifts in certain ways. Once you decide on that, make sure you follow this plan - no matter what. If you want to succeed you need to be sure that you are prepared for every possibility and that you also have an exit plan in case things go south.

2. Analyze your coins

Remember that the cryptocurrency market today is a bear market. It's going through its rough patches, but it will emerge from this one day. Therefore, make sure your coins are consolidated. Separate coins that have long term value from those that don't and cut them out accordingly.

3. Don't listen to skeptics

Since there is a lot of negative talk surrounding
cryptocurrency and its future, it is easy to get
influenced and affected by skeptics. The important
thing to remember is to block this negative noise and
not to let it affect your trading decisions. There will
always be pessimists but that does not mean you give
up on what you believe in.

4. Find teammates

It can be great fun trading cryptocurrency, if you are
surrounded by the right people. Get in touch with your
friends who are as crazy about crypto trading as you are
and share information with each other. You may even
want to establish connections globally through
cryptocurrency forums where you can get authentic
news and trends on cryptocurrencies.

5. Use trading tools

These days a lot of tools are readily available that allow
you to trade after thoroughly examining and analyzing
the market. Don't be afraid to use these tools to your
advantage. Popular tools include Trading View pro,
Hacked.com, and signalgroups.com.

What are the benefits of crypto trading?

Here are a few of the many benefits of cryptocurrency trading:
1. Volatility
Cryptocurrency markets are extremely volatile which may be seen by some as a downside but that is what makes cryptocurrency trading so exciting and fun. While the chance of incurring a loss is high, the chance of gaining a huge profit is equally high.

2. Trading hours

Cryptocurrency markets run 24 hours, there is no set time to trade which makes them accessible. Since there is no centralized governance, you can trade wherever and whenever you want. The only time a market might be unavailable, is when it's getting infrastructural updates or forks.

3. Improved liquidity

Improved liquidity means that you can convert your cryptocurrency into cash quickly and without impacting the market price of the currency. Improved liquidity also means better pricing, faster transactions and greater accuracy in analysis.

4. Easy movement

Cryptocurrency trading allows you to go long or short without any barriers. Your movement is absolutely free, and it is completely up to you what choices you make.

What is the best cryptocurrency trading platform?

There are many cryptocurrency trading platforms, some of the more popular ones include:
1. Kraken
If you are a beginner, then this exchange is perfect for you. It will guide you and help you to become an expert in trading.
2. Bitfinex
For those looking to track interested buyers and sellers for their particular financial instrument, then Bitfinex is the best option. The software offers advanced tracking capabilities and has almost eight variations in order typeset for all scenario sets, making it unique.
3. Bittrex
Bittrex's main aim is to cut the transaction time and process it faster. Its cutting-edge technology can increase the demand for cryptocurrency and in terms of security, it is safer than most platforms.

What is the best way to day trade cryptocurrency?

Day trading is when you trade your currency on the same day and can be either very profitable or non-profitable. Day trading platforms worth mentioning include:

1. BitMex

While BitMex only allows you to trade Bitcoin, it is one of the earliest platforms and was launched in 2014. No fees are charged on deposits and withdrawals of Bitcoins on this site, making it user-friendly. The interface is very simple and only allows users to keep one type of account. It is uncomplicated and fuss-free.

2. CEX.IO

This platform allows you to trade your currency against multiple fiat options such as USD, EUR, and GBP, etc. It offers both, a traditional trading platform which is simply buying and selling for fiat, as well as an advanced trading platform that allows you to set limits and engage in margin trading.

3. Whaleclub

This is another day trading platform that is popular amongst day traders. It only allows you to trade in cryptocurrency. All deposits and withdrawals are also in digital currency. It doesn't charge for account activity and deposits, however, there is a small fee for withdrawals. Overall, it's very specific in its trading and is easy to use.

How does the IRS treat cryptocurrency?

The IRS treats cryptocurrencies as property. Which means that if you are just holding cryptocurrency without any value being added or subtracted, then you incur no taxes. If you hold the currency for less than one year then you owe a short-term capital gains tax and if you own it for more than a year then you owe a long term capital gains tax.
Other taxable events include: if you sell your cryptocurrency, trade it for another currency, or if you purchase something with that cryptocurrency then you have to pay taxes. If your cryptocurrency sells at a profit, you then owe a capitals gain tax.

Chapter 7 Strategies For Making Money In Cryptocurrency

A trading strategy involves buying and selling cryptocurrency assets using predefined rules.
A good trading strategy should have a well-thought-out plan with specific trading objectives, a trading timeframe, and a risk tolerance plan.
The plan involves developing methods aimed at buying and selling crypto assets. It should also have a strategy that meets your investment goals. Trading strategies help identify the entry and exit points in the crypto market.

Cryptocurrency Investment Strategies

Buy & Hold
Buy and hold (sometimes referred to as HODL) is the basic trading strategy where you buy the crypto asset, hold it, and later sell it. To hold the asset requires a lot of confidence. You have to be optimistic about the rising prices to hold the asset and sell at a higher price later. The investor holds the asset as long as the prices are rising. The bull market fuels the buy and hold strategy.
HODL means "Hold On For Dear Life" and has been used in the Bitcoin crypto-sphere to indicate the buy and hold strategy for cryptocurrency investments. Holding the coin for a certain period can result in long-term benefits to the crypto traders.

Many HODL investors have been able to achieve their long-term business goals. Investing in multiple cryptocurrencies such as Ethereum, EOS, Ripple, etc is one way to diversify the investment risks.

As cryptocurrencies increase in value, the gains are not as large as they are for lower-priced cryptocurrencies. Right now, an investor can buy almost 50 Ethereum for the same price as 1 Bitcoin. This spread varies, at the Bitcoin/Ethereum price peak, it was about 20:1. Diversifying the cryptocurrency portfolio can result in better returns and also re-balance the portfolio.

Most Buy and Hold investors do not set a stop-loss. A stop-loss would set a sell order if the price dropped an amount that is uncomfortable for the investor. However, setting a stop-loss removes the emotion from the trade. It locks in the loss but prevents an even larger loss by a stubborn investor. Setting stops to limit the downside is recommended by most successful investors.

Advantages of the Buy and Hold Strategy in a Bull Market

1. Reduces market noise by 95%
The long-term bull trend line helps bolster the buy and hold trading strategy since it reduces the market noise brought up by a lower trading term. Short-term trading patterns are usually unpredictable, which can affect trades. A weekly chart line on price actions is non-volatile for a certain period.

2.Reduced transaction costs
- Long-term traders using the buy and hold method do not over-trade. This technique

significantly reduces transaction costs. On the other hand, a short-term trader engaged in weekly or daily trades has to account for each trade's accumulated transaction cost as well.

- Trading on several short-term trades will be very expensive compared to executing a few long-term trades.

3.Reduces psychological strain

- Executing several short-term or medium-term trades can be very stressful, especially if the trader is less experienced. The buy and hold method is less stressful than short-term trades. While it can still be stressful, the buy and hold method is much better than the short trading strategy.

4. Perfect market timing is not important

- The buy and hold strategy is attractive to many traders because market timing is not important. Traders can enter into the market without being on guard for a major pullback against an incoming bull market trend. Long-term investors know that they can miss potential opportunities if they rely on perfect market timing.

5. Time efficiency

- The buy and hold trading method is ideal for investors aiming for higher gains with minimal time expenditure. Long-term investors don't have to constantly monitor price changes daily or use technical analysis charts to watch price movements. Still, they should always keep track of fundamental news in the cryptocurrency market and check their position every so often to benefit from their crypto-asset investment.

6. Lower taxes

- Holding crypto assets for a long period results in great capital gains. Investments held at least a year before selling are eligible for lower taxes. The assets attract long-term tax rates instead of higher short-term rates.

7. Dollar-Cost Averaging

- A Buy and Hold investor will typically invest on a regular schedule like each week or each month. Many investors buy $100 of Bitcoin every month. As the price goes up and down, the result is averaged. If the long term trend is a bull market, the investor will see an increase in their assets.

Tips For Successful HODL Cryptocurrency Trading

- Traders should use a large time frame like weekly and monthly charts to perform technical analysis.
- Watch out for the factors that influence long-term goals of Bitcoin trading.

- Taking advantage of the pullback strategy will enable you to obtain a better entry price point.
- Avoid holding leveraged crypto coins for a long time since it can be costly. If used, minimize the leverage.
- When using stop-loss orders, you should not place it too close to the entry.
- Dollar-cost average to even out the high and low price fluctuations.

Investors using HODL should guard their investments against potential market crashes and understand how to take advantage of the bull market to utilize profits and cut losses. These investors can benefit from understanding the techniques in this book.

Bitcoin Mining Strategy

The process of creating new coins is called mining. Mining Bitcoin (or other crypto coins) is another way to obtain coins. Unfortunately, Bitcoin mining has progressed to the point where custom hardware "rigs" are needed.

However, you can mine less popular coins using second-hand rigs and exchange the coins for Bitcoin on the exchange website. You can also hold the coins for a while and sell when the price increases.

Miners have the expense of buying an operating the rigs. In some cases, this can be a significant cost in electricity and cooling costs since the rigs create heat while running.

Arbitraging Strategy

In an arbitrage strategy, you buy the coins at a lower price and sell them at a higher price in a different location. As an example, the price of Bitcoin is $8500 on Coinbase and $8600 on Binance. Buying 1 Bitcoin on Coinbase and then selling 1 Bitcoin on Binance could return a profit of $100 minus the Binance and Coinbase fees.

This is less viable now because the technique is now widely known. Some companies and people are constantly scanning for price discrepancies and are more likely to act quickly than you.

However, this may be a good technique with less well-known coins.

Passive Income from Dividend Payouts Strategy

I hesitated before including this strategy because there have been many scams around "renting" your coins. Do your homework on the companies that advertise dividends because the vast majority of these have been scams that take your cryptocurrency and leave you with nothing.

I'm including it here because it is a viable strategy if you use a reputable company.

In some cases, lending cryptocurrency coins can earn dividends between 5% and 10% per year. These dividends are usually limited to a few coins like Bitcoin, NEO, and VeChain. If the coin price goes up for a certain period, you gain more profits.

Recently, coins that use Proof-of-Stake instead of Proof-of-Work can earn dividends while held in cryptocurrency exchanges such as Coinbase, Bittrex, or Kraken.

Trading Strategy

Trading is the primary theme of this book so this chapter will focus more on trading than the other strategies.

Long Trade

A long trade is a term used when purchasing cryptocurrency assets at a cheaper price with the expectation of selling them at a high price in the future to gain profit.

Day traders can also use a long trade strategy when they buy the asset with the expectation that the price will rise during the day and then sell. "Buy" and "long" are common terms in the trading sector. If an investor says, "Going long," it means he or she has an interest in buying a particular asset and holding onto it with the expectation that it will increase in value.

Long trades have unlimited profit gains since the price of the coin can go up indefinitely.

Short Trade

In a short trade, the coin is sold because the trader expects the price to decrease. If the coin isn't owned, traders can borrow the coin for a fee. This is called a "naked" short and is only recommended for experienced traders since the price could go up.

In a "naked" short trade, the trader sells the borrowed coin to repurchase it later at a lower price and return the coin to the person it was borrowed from. If the selling price is higher than what they repurchase it at, they keep the profit.

Short sales have high financial risks. Be very careful when using this strategy because sometimes key market players can drive the price up, forcing short position speculators to buy back the asset before the price goes too high. This is referred to as a "short squeeze" and ironically, this can cause the price to zoom even higher since there are more buyers.

Typical Trading Strategies

It is hard to determine when prices are at a peak or valley, but you can use the following strategies to take advantage of the bull and bear markets.

Choosing A Trading Timeframe

Trading charts are drawn on different timeframes or even sometimes with other data like price range or the number of trades made. Charts can show minute, hourly, daily, or weekly data. Based on your needs and the type of cryptocurrency used, you can choose either a long timeframe or a short timeframe. The trading timeframe chosen depends on your personality.

If you want to make many trades within a single day, you can choose a short time frame. If you only do one or two trades per week, then you can choose a longer time frame.

Long Term Traders

Long-term traders rely on either daily or weekly charts to make trading decisions. Weekly trading charts identify the long-term trends and help set the trading plan. In this form of trading, you don't have to monitor price changes throughout the day.

The daily charts are useful for determining the entry and exit points, while a monthly chart can be used to determine the primary market trend. Traders and investors will also have enough time to evaluate each trade before taking action.

Day Traders

A daily trader can rely on 5, 15, or 60-minute charts to identify the primary market trend. The five-minute charts indicate a short-term trend. These charts show the specific points where traders should take action and enter or exit the trend market.

Traders using the day trading strategy always have to be tuned in. Not doing so can negatively impact your profitability. For this reason, brokers and other third-party firms offer user-friendly apps accessible via mobile devices.

Day trading is a short-term trading technique where you can hold the asset for a few hours and sell it with the hopes of getting positive returns. Chart analysis allows traders to monitor the price movement of the cryptocurrency and predict future direction based on its historical data.

Day Trading

Cryptocurrency day trading involves buying and selling crypto assets at a profit. The practice has become popular in recent years due to high volatility and trading volumes.

Daily crypto trading is characterized by high risk. Before you enter into any trade, you have to know where to take profits. You also need to know the price to stop the trade to avoid major losses. Smart investors control the size of their position in the market. They also do not risk a significant portion of their investment portfolio or use too much leverage in a single trade.

To succeed in day trading, you have to be tuned in constantly. Receiving any big news or announcements just a few minutes later than everyone else can result in huge profits or losses.

Types of Day Traders

Day traders use different approaches to achieve their trading goals. They can either be speculators or technical analysts.
Speculators
The speculators find the outside factors that influence the price of the cryptocurrency. They look for indicators such as news events to predict the gain or loss of cryptocurrency asset values.
There are several user-friendly mobile apps designed to ensure you're constantly updated about what's happening in the cryptocurrency world. As a speculator, you have to spend a considerable amount of time on your preferred cryptocurrency platform daily and cryptocurrency news sites, so choose an app that meets your investment needs and trading style.
Technical Analysts
Technical analysis is more concerned about the market itself than any external influences affecting asset pricing. Technical analyst traders use financial charts and patterns to predict price movement. Learning how to use technical analysis tools will give you a better idea of the direction of coin prices. Knowing how to read chart lines and patterns is very important for any day trader.

A day trading strategy is not a get-rich-quick scheme. It has many risks, and you are likely to lose a lot of money before fully understanding how the strategy works. Even experienced traders prefer making small profits over a large number of trades with this method.

When buying cryptocurrencies, you need to compare the different types of brokers and what they offer. Select brokers who offer cryptocurrency trades with lower fees for frequent trading because day trades have many trades in a day and the fees can erode profitable trades.

Getting Started in Day Trading

After deciding to day trading, you need to choose a home exchange for your currency. When choosing a home exchange, remember that different exchanges provide different fee structures, have various minimum trade restrictions, and offer different coin pairings.

The fee structure influences the volume of trade. If your trading style involves trading in large volumes, you may only get small profits from the trade, since part of the profit will pay for the trading fees.

Once you have registered your account for daily trading, develop a trading strategy. Research the coin you want to invest in, as well as any relevant news or technical analysis about it and its market.

Set ground rules for day trading. For example, set a rule that restricts you from risking more than 1% of your predetermined investment on a single trade. Successful day trading requires discipline; without it, you will incur huge losses.

Set stop-loss limits. A stop-loss limit is an important factor when setting up a trading strategy, and it acts as your exit strategy. Setting the limit to a particular level will allow your exchange program to automatically exit the trade after attaining that level. If you buy 0.01 Bitcoin for $100, you can set the stop loss to $80. This will ensure you don't lose more than 20% of your investment by automatically selling the coins to preserve 80% of your investment in case the coin price falls. One thing to note is that during a panic, there will be a lot of people trying to sell and the stop loss may sell at a lower price than you selected. Luckily panics are rare events but they need to be considered a part of day trading.

You can also limit the sell orders. This will automatically close a trade once the coin reaches a price level you select. If the coin price is on an upward trend and you bought 0.01 Bitcoin for $100, you can set a sell limit order to $130 to ensure you lock in the gains. Setting the limit order will ensure the coin is sold automatically when the price level reaches $130 which would be a 30% profit. It is always good to have an exit value in mind when you make a trade.

Don't second guess yourself if the price continues higher, a profit is always a win.

Trading volatility

Volatility describes the change in prices of an asset - either moving up or down very quickly. The price direction can result in higher gains or losses to traders. The prices are sensitive to regulatory changes and highly dependent on daily crypto news and announcements.

Bitcoin prices can rise and fall anywhere from 5% to 50% within a single day, whereas the prices of traditional markets such as the New York Stock Exchange (NYSE) typically do not change as much in the same timeframe. Trading volatility is a distinguishing factor between day trading cryptocurrency and day trading other general assets. Traditional day traders typically sell their positions before the stock market closes since news after the close can have a large impact. Although cryptocurrency exchanges are open 24 hours a day, 7 days a week, limiting the holding window is a good habit for crypto traders as well.

Traders can take advantage of the volatile market and make good returns on their investments, but doing so involves a keen willingness to make risky moves and accept high losses.

Day Trading Taxes

The taxes paid on Bitcoin assets depend on the length of time you held the asset. Different countries have different tax laws that govern different tax views on cryptocurrency assets. Therefore, perform due diligence and follow the tax laws for your country.

In the United States, if you hold a crypto asset for less than a year, the transaction will be taxed at your normal income tax rate. When you buy crypto assets with fiat currency, you're not liable to pay taxes on the purchase transaction (until it is sold).

When you sell cryptocurrency assets, you have to pay income tax for every sell transaction. By default, you are taxed using the First In First Out (FIFO) method. In the FIFO method, your first sale will be matched to the price of the first purchase and you will pay tax on the amount of gain. There is also a Last In First Out (LIFO) method that may affect taxes so consult a tax professional.

If you hold a Bitcoin asset for more than a year, it will be classified as a capital gain under US tax laws and the asset will be taxed at a lower rate (currently 15%). Capital gain taxes are typically lower than most people's regular income taxes. Most day traders won't be able to use this lower tax rate because they buy and sell so frequently.

Day Trading Considerations

1.Volatility

- Day trading cryptocurrency prices move up and down quickly and can either lead to higher profits or loss, unlike stock asset prices. The price of a coin can rise and fall 10% to 50% or even more in a single day.

2.Accept losses
- Day trading Bitcoin or any other cryptocurrency may not work as expected. Sometimes you have losses while others make profits. You need to accept losses once they occur; this is part of trading. You will not make the correct prediction every time, and even the most experienced traders make wrong predictions.

- If you have losses, don't try to recover it by taking even higher risks. This will lead to failure. You should always accept losses and then evaluate what went wrong and course-correct for the next transaction.

3.Practice first

- Before investing in real money, you need to practice first. Although not all exchange platforms offer you a demo account, the CryptoHopper and Coins2Learn platforms provide a trading simulator to practice trading. The platforms give tips to new traders on how to be successful in trading. Keep in mind that they make money with the up-sell so you will get a lot of emails, etc.
- You can paper trade using a notebook to track when you buy and sell and at what prices. Once you are satisfied that you understand the market, go ahead and invest with real money.
- When beginning to trade, it's recommended to start with small amounts. That is, an amount you can afford to lose since paper trading/simulation doesn't prepare you for real-world losses.

- As you continue trading, you will hone your skills along with a better understanding of the highs and lows of the trending market.

4.Set targets
- After learning how the market works and its ups and downs, you can set targets for yourself. You need a plan for your expectations at the end of the day. Targets should be focused - such as how much of a loss you can absorb, how much of a gain before selling, how long to stay in a trade, and a safe stop-loss value.

- Day trading has short-term gains which can be as low as 1% per trade. Several gains each day can increase your bank amount and help you build a steady income.

5.Use Stop-losses

- Stop-losses are an essential factor in day trading cryptocurrency. A stop-loss is a value set so that if you were expecting the price to increase but the coin price drops to that stop-loss point, you automatically exit the trade. It is used to prevent more losses.
- If you bought Bitcoin for $6000, you can set a stop-loss at 10%. Then, if the price of Bitcoin drops to $5400, the system automatically sells the investment on your behalf. If you're not online when the prices drop, the stop-loss will save you from incurring further losses automatically.
- You can also use limit sell orders, which allow the system to automatically sell your Bitcoin or close a trade after Bitcoin hits the set higher price. In this case, if you set a limit sell order to 10%, the coin will automatically be sold when the price hit $6600.

6.Choose appropriate trading bots

- Based on your trading needs, choose a trading bot that helps you become more successful. Compare different trading bots in terms of their reputation, fees, cost, features, and other essential factors based on your desired use.
- Note: When day trading, you have to be calm throughout despite the rushed timeframes. You should keep the following in mind:
- You shouldn't be greedy

- Don't trade an amount you're not ready to lose

- Don't move from one strategy to another. You should always evaluate your success and failure before making any changes otherwise you are not learning from your successes and losses.

Bull & Bear Market

A bull market occurs when crypto asset prices are expected to rise during a particular trading period. In the stock market, the prices of securities rise and fall continuously over a particular trading term. The bull market indicates that the prices of various securities are rising for an extended period, usually over months or years.

The upward trend results in higher gains in the crypto market. In a bull market, investors buy more coins to increase their profits.

Although it is difficult to predict changes in market trends, investors relying on bull markets are confident and optimistic about higher returns for an extended period. A bull market is characterized by higher highs and lower lows - a concept that is explained in more detail later in this book.

In the stock market, a bull market is an indicator of expansion in the economy. Typically economic conditions affect the prices of security assets traded.

Cryptocurrency is seen as a safe haven and many times, bad economic data will result in Bitcoin and other cryptocurrencies increasing in price. This is another reason that cryptocurrency is good to have in your portfolio for diversity.

Investors can take advantage of a bull market by buying crypto assets when prices start to rise and selling them when the price is at its peak.

A bear market is characterized by a period of downward price movement. The price falling results in a downward trend.

In a cryptocurrency bear market, traders are more likely to sell their assets than purchase additional ones. During this trading term, you can expect to see both lower highs and lower lows in the trend lines.

Tips for Cryptocurrency Trading

Have a purpose for each trade
Before placing any trade, you need to have a reason as to why you want to trade crypto assets. In the cryptocurrency market, there is always a winner and a loser. It is a zero-sum game; for every win, there is a corresponding loss.

Whether you're a day trader or long-term trader, you must be patient. Don't rush a trade and cause losses. sometimes it's better to make a small gain than rush into losses with a single trade.

Set profit targets and stop-loss orders
You should always know when to enter and exit the market and how much profit you want to make. If you plan to get out of the market when you make a certain profit or if the price hits a set target, stick to that plan. Don't be greedy.

Place stop-loss orders to help you cut down on losses. When trading, put emotions aside and set a stop-loss point so that when the price drops to the stop-loss points, the asset is sold automatically.

Manage Risks

You need to learn how to manage risk in the business. It's better to accumulate a low amount of profit from small, regular trades than to risk everything by investing big. If the market is less liquid, invest small amounts and set both stop-loss and profit targets further from the buying price.

Welcome FOMO

FOMO (fear of missing out) is trading psychology experienced by traders and one of the reasons why the majority of traders fail. There are times when almost everyone wants to trade, and you feel like jumping into the market by buying the coins. Bitcoin whales are watching every move that small traders are making. This will lead to an oversupply of coins in the market, and the price will drop as demand vanishes.

If you can harness your emotions, you can exploit the FOMO and sell when you see that people are in FOMO mode.

Don't Buy Because The Price Is Low

Buying coins because the price is low is one common mistake made by beginning traders. You need to look for other factors before buying the coin. You shouldn't base the decision to buy the coin on its affordability. You should look at the market cap of the coin. The higher the cap, the more suitable to invest in it.

Volatile Market Condition Created Through Underlying Assets

The Bitcoin price is quite volatile, and it affects the prices of other currencies. If the price of Bitcoin rises, the price of altcoins and other coins may drop since the available money is flowing into Bitcoin.

The variability of Bitcoin prices confuses traders, making it difficult to understand the market. In this case, you can set profit targets and rely on them to sell or just hold your coins while you wait for a clear market.

Be Vigilant Of ICOs

Some startups encourage the public to invest in their ICO (Initial Coin Offering) with a promise to get promoted coins at lower prices to sell at a profit. ICO's higher returns attract a large number of investors. Recently a large number of firms using ICO strategies are scams. Therefore, be careful when investing in an ICO.

Scrutinize all information provided to attract investors. Do a background check on the people behind that firm, and analyze them to see whether they can deliver as promised. Don't just buy because of the returns they're promising.

Diversify your investment

Although cryptocurrency investments can offer large returns, they're very unpredictable. A slight change in the market conditions can make them fall within a day. You can also lose everything you hold in just seconds, especially if the exchange platform is hacked. Diversification will allow you to cope with this uncertainty.

Chapter 8 Wallets & Security

One of the most important topics about Cryptocurrencies is one of the less researched. There are many ways to store and secure Cryptocurrencies, and we will take a look at each possibility and its advantages or disadvantages. You have to keep in mind that a Cryptocurrency is a purely digital asset; therefore, the one controlling your private key has unlimited access to your assets. It is crucial for us to emphasize the importance of this topic. Similar to your bank account the main rule is, protect your PIN / private key and only share it with the ones you can trust 100%.

What is a Wallet?

A wallet can be imagined as a way to save your private keys. You will probably remember that you access your assets with a private key which is connected to your stake of coins in the network. There are different ways of securing that private key, and that is what we call a wallet. The user has several means of securing its private key, such as "paper wallet", "soft wallet", "hard wallet", "mind wallets", "exchanges" and the difference between "hot wallets" and "cold wallets".

Cold Wallets

The so-called "cold wallet" is every type of wallet where the private key is stored offline, with no connection to the internet.

Paper Wallet

A paper wallet is probably the most secure way to store coins but at the same time the most inconvenient. A paper wallet is nothing else than creating a private key and writing it down on a piece of paper.
(There are a couple of fundamental things for you to take care of when storing coins like this:
- Generate the private key by yourself and do NOT use an online generator.
- Write the private key with your hand in clear patterns, with water and heat proof pencil. Remember this key might have to "survive" years or decades.
- Do NOT print it out, your printer or computer might save it.
- Make more than one copy and distribute them at different places. In case of a robbery, natural catastrophe or others.
- Do NOT save the key on any electronic device.)

If you follow these rules, your private cannot be stolen easily. This type of storage is very safe, but unfortunately very inconvenient because you cannot access your wallet quickly. Theoretically, you have to change the private seed every time you are entering the private key, in case of spy software. In which degree this is relevant for you, lays within your responsibility. You can save the public address on your computer without any doubt, as we learned already, knowing the public address does not reveal your private key.

Brain Wallet

A brain wallet means you remember the private key and therefore do not need any copy of it. To be honest, it is doubtful that regular people can remember a private key, because usually, they are quite long. The risk of forgetting your private key is very high, and then there is no way of recovering it.

Hot Wallets

These are the wallets which are saved on a device with internet connection. Hot wallets do not have to be insecure, but it is essential to understand their risks because today you need to expect that everything can be hacked.

Soft Wallet

Soft wallets are a very popular way of saving the private keys. They describe software which serves as a safe for your private key, where you need to come up with a password to protect it. It is important to know that theoretically your computer can be hacked; therefore, the password of the soft wallet should not be saved anywhere on the computer as well.
(For your safety, we advise you to write down your private key on an extra paper, just like a paper wallet.) In case your device is broken, you can easily access your coins if you made a backup of your private key. If not, your coins are lost. Therefore, it is vital to ALWAYS have a backup plan -think about the "What if".

Hard Wallet

A hard wallet is a combination of a cold wallet and a hot wallet. This type of wallet was created by companies such as Ledger or Trezor, which created a wallet that can be compared to an USB-Stick. Even if it looks similar, it is not an ordinary one, as you need to enter a PIN code to access the wallet and all of the private keys on it.
The company Ledger, for example, does have a backup of every data saved on your wallet; therefore, it is possible to restore it even if it was destroyed. (It does have pros and cons, at this point we do not want to say whether it is good or bad that they create backups).
The speciality of Trezor is that you are required to touch the device AND enter the PIN to enter your assets.

Other manufacturers of hard wallets do not offer this service, but it is essential to know that Ledger has this characteristic. Besides, even here it is important to create a paper wallet as a backup in case you lose your data.

Exchanges

Exchanges are the most popular way of storing coins because it is the most convenient way. If you store your coins on an exchange, you can easily trade them and send them anywhere you want. This is due to the reason that the exchange administers your private keys for you. However, this method of storing coins is highly risky. Remember you are not directly in possession of the private key which means, that if the exchange is hacked, you can lose your coins. This is the main reason why many people think a blockchain can be hacked or hackers can easily steal your coins. It is true that in 2017 a couple of exchanges were hacked and a lot of money has been stolen, but this was not because Cryptocurrencies are hard to store. This was due to the reason that many people did not care about storing possibilities.

Deterministic Wallets

When you are using a hot wallet, your public address may change from time to time. You might have recognised that some exchanges enable the possibility to generate a new address (or you were afraid that your coins are lost because you sent them to the wrong address). First of all, this mechanism is nothing to be scared of!
(This technology is called "deterministic wallets" and is a feature which aims to improve security. Let's take the IOTA light Wallet as an example. The first thing you do is to choose a "seed" which contains (in IOTAs case) 24 words. These words can be chosen randomly and are now the seed of your private keys. Based on that the wallet creates a first private key and a public address, where you can receive coins. The next time you enter your wallet, you can recreate a public address, or it changes automatically. The reason is that based on your first private key and in connection to your seed the wallet calculates a new private key where you can receive coins now. To access all of the private keys which were generated, your wallet calculates the following keys and sums up the total of your balance.)
This procedure provides a higher security standard because your coins are now split. It is, as we already learnt, impossible to "hack" a private key, but in case someone guesses it right or steals the original one from a digital copy, he cannot steal the total amount of money. Even if a private key is given out twice (that could theoretically happen, but it is more likely to win the lottery five times in a row and then die by the hit of a bolt of lightning) you would only lose a part of your money.

How should I secure my assets?

There are a couple of important rules to follow, and it is essential for you to think about the best way to store your assets.

First, it is crucial that you choose your wallet depending on your requirements. That means, if you are into day trading you have different demands than someone who is willing to hold the assets for years. Be aware of the risks that come with exchange possessing your private keys.

Moreover, be aware that some shitcoins can have wallets which contain viruses. Therefore, it is essential that you research the Cryptocurrency and evaluate if it is trustworthy or not. You should avoid downloading any programs or contents with an uncertain background!

It cannot be repeated often enough - you need to have a backup plan. Store your access to your wallets, exchanges or ledgers in different geographical places and secure them against robbery, natural catastrophes and so on.

Generally, there is no best way to store Crypto assets. In the following paragraph, we will discuss some safety measures. Whether you follow them and to which extent lays within your responsibility.

VPN

A VPN is a Virtual Private Network - a way to secure
your IP address by giving you temporarily a new IP.
That means hackers and online providers are not able
to see where the signal is coming from. The background
is that hackers might be able to access your home
network through your IP address or collect personal
data.
Hackers are searching for wallet connections to find the
user. A wallet has a unique pattern of small data
transactions with the blockchain - those could be
detected and could identify your IP.
A VPN is distracting potential hackers from your assets
and makes it hard for them to allocate your position
and network. Even though VPNs are a good additional
security measure that does not mean that you and your
assets are at risk if you are not using a VPN.

2FA

2FA or two-factor-authenticator is a must have!
Regardless of the exchange you use, you should always
enable the 2FA. The google authenticator, for example,
is an application which generates a new password every
20 seconds and is linked to your account.
(This software is based on a TOTP protocol, meaning
Temporary One Time Password. The most famous and
secure app is the "Google Authenticator". We highly
recommend using it instead of SMS 2FA.)

Chapter 9 Laws Of Creating A Bitcoin Account

Bitcoin is registered to Bitcoin wallet address in the block chain. Creating a Bitcoin wallet address is as easy within few minutes. But to be able to spend your bitcoin in your wallet the owner must know the corresponding key and digitally sign these transactions. The network signs the signature using the public key.

Bitcoin mining:

Mining of bitcoin is a record keeping service done through the use of computer processing power. Miners keep the block chain consistent, complete and unalterable by repeatedly grouping every broadcast transaction into a block which is then broadcast to the network and verified by recipient nodes.

The system used in mining is based on Adam Back's 1997 anti-spam scheme, Hash cash. The proof-of-work (POW) requires miners to find a number called a nonce, so that when the block content is hashed along with the nonce, the result is numerically smaller than the network's difficulty target. The POW along with the chaining of blocks makes modifying the block chain very hard, as an attacker must modify all the previous blocks in order for the modification of one block to be accepted. And as new blocks are mined all the time, the difficulty of modifying a block increases as time passes as the number of subsequent blocks increases.

Supply of bitcoin

All successful miners who find the new block are rewarded with newly created bitcoin and transaction fees. To claim the reward, a special transaction called coin base is included with the processed payments.

The bitcoin network was designed such that the reward given to miners for adding a block will be halved approximately every four years. As times goes on the reward will decrease to zero and the limit of 21 million bitcoins will be reached, then the miners will be rewarded by transaction fee only. The inventors of bitcoin design a maximum limit of 21 million bitcoins to be ever mined thus generating an artificial scarcity in the nearest future leading to higher increase in bitcoin value.

Bitcoin Wallet:

A bitcoin wallet is like a bank which stores bitcoins, due to the nature of the system bitcoins is inseparable from the block chain transaction ledger. A bitcoin wallet stores the digital credentials for your bitcoin holdings and allows one to receive and send bitcoin.

Chapter 10 How You Can Purchase Your Bitcoin Online?

Haven learned about the basics of bitcoin, and you feel like purchasing some bitcoins. Bitcoin can be bought on exchanges or directly from other people, can also get them from debits cards to wire transfers or even with other crypto currencies. In this chapter we discuss some steps you can use to get your bitcoin.

Set up a wallet account

The wallet account enables you to store your bitcoin after purchase notwithstanding your mode of purchase. It can be an online wallet that can be part of an exchange platform or via an independent provider. It can also be a desktop wallet, a mobile wallet or an offline one like a hardware device or a paper wallet). The most important aspects of a wallet are safeguarding your keys and passwords safe. Losing your password or key may risk you losing access to the bitcoin stored there.

Open an account at an exchange and buy bitcoin online Once you grant the exchanges company permission they can buy and sell bitcoin on your behalf. There are over hundreds of bitcoin exchanges currently operating globally, hence it's very important for one to make a thorough research about the exchange company before investing your money, some few examples for Bitcoin Exchanges Company Are Coin base, Bit stamp, and Polonies.

Most exchanges company do request for identification for account setup due to the clampdown on known-Your-Client (KYC) and anti-money-laundering (AML) regulation.

Some exchanges do accept payment through bank transfer or credit card while few accept PayPal transfers. Upon receiving your payment by the exchange company, hey will purchase the corresponding amount of bitcoin on your behalf and deposit them in an automatically generated wallet on the exchange.

Purchasing bitcoin with cash

Bitcoins can also be purchase worth cash using some platform. Platforms like LocalBicoins will assist you to find buyers and seller of bitcoins near you who are willing to exchange bitcoin for cash. While in the United States platforms like LibertyXhelps in listing out retails outlets who you can exchange cash for bitcoin easily. Also, platforms like WallofCoins, Playful, and Bit Quick will direct you to a bank near you that will allow you to make a cash deposit and receive bitcoin a few hours later.

Bitcoin ATMs are machines that easily receive and also send through your bitcoin wallet in exchange for cash. Bitcoin ATMs also operate in different ways similar to bank ATMs you feed in the bills, hold your wallet's QR code up to a screen and the corresponding amount of bitcoin are stag to your account. Coinatmradar can be used to place the closest ATM closer to you.

Chapter 11 Cryptocurrency Trading Broker

As a cryptocurrency investor/trader, it is important that you work with a reliable and trustworthy trading broker. If you do a search online, you will easily find so many brokers that seem to offer you the same service. But, how do you know which of these brokers will best suit your needs? Here are the standards to look for:

Trading platform

Your broker is the one that will provide you with the platform that you can use to buy and sell, as well as open trading positions. Hence, your broker should provide you with a professional-looking platform. Although the design of the platform may not be as important as its features, it is still beneficial to have a professionally designed platform as to help set the right mood for trading/investing. Your broker should also provide you with tools such as graphs that can help you come up with a sound trading decision. Simply put, the trading platform should make the experience of trading cryptocurrencies easy and convenient for you. You should also check the different cryptocurrencies traded by your broker. Of course, the more cryptocurrencies are available for trading, the more choices that you will have.

Customer support

It is important that you work with a broker that has an active and professional customer support team. The customer support can help you in case you have questions and especially if you are having technical issues. Your broker will provide you with ways on how you can get in touch with the customer support team. Normally, an email address would be provided or a certain page on the platform may be used where you can directly send a message to the support team. A live on-page chat service may also be provided by your broker. Sometimes a broker may even provide you with a number that you can call to reach the customer support team.

It is suggested that you test the customer support to see how responsive it is. A good way of doing this is by testing the support team. Just send an inquiry and pay attention to how fast and professional it responds. You should be able to get a response within 24 hours. In your life as a cryptocurrency investor/trader, it is important for you to work only with a trading broker that has an active and professional customer support team.

Latest reviews

Just like when looking for other services or products online, you should also read the latest reviews given to the trading broker that you intend to use. Be sure to read the reviews before you make any form of deposit. Also, do not rely on just one website for reviews. This is because many cryptocurrency trading brokers hire writers to come up with a positive write-up about their business. Hence, read as many reviews as you can. It is also good if you can read some negative reviews. This usually shows that the reviews are honest and true. To find the reviews on a particular broker, simply open your browser, type the name of the broker, and add the word "reviews." The SERP will then give you a list of related pages. Also, pay attention to the dates when the reviews were written.

Mobile version

These days, it is much faster and convenient to access the Internet through your mobile phone. Trading brokers are well aware of this, and so many of them provide a mobile feature or version of the trading platform. All legitimate and high-quality cryptocurrency trading brokers offer a mobile version of their trading platform, so this is something that you should not worry about.

The mobile version should be easy and convenient to use. Although it may not provide all the features that you can enjoy when you use a desktop computer, it should at least provide you with the important parts of the trading platform. You should be able to manage your account easily, as well as open and close trading positions. It should also allow you to make deposits and withdrawals easily. Last but not least, it should be easy to use and navigate. Again, your trading broker should help you and make the experience of trading more convenient and interesting.

Deposit and withdrawal limits and requirements

Check the minimum and maximum deposit and withdrawal requirements of your broker. Also, keep in mind that making a deposit is usually easier than making a withdrawal. Normally, making a deposit can be made instantly provided you transfer funds from your wallet into your trading account. However, when making a withdrawal, most brokers will require you to first submit some documents, such as a valid ID and a proof of billing, before it would process your withdrawal request. This is where the problem actually starts. Some people fail to make a successful withdrawal. Therefore, before you deposit anything into your trading account, be sure to be clear with your broker regarding its requirements for making a successful withdrawal; otherwise, you may risk having your funds and profits locked in your account without any way of withdrawing them. Be sure that you have the required documents in your possession, and make sure that they are still valid and have not yet expired. If you have questions or more concerns on this matter, do not hesitate to contact the customer support team.

Additional notes:

It is fast and easy to sign up for a trading account with a cryptocurrency trading broker. The process usually takes just around two minutes. The important thing is identifying which broker that you will use. Be careful because there are scammers out there who are always looking for their next victim. Hence, make sure that you work only with a reliable and trustworthy cryptocurrency trading broker.

Now, if you just want to purchase bitcoin or any other known cryptocurrencies and make a long-term investment, it should be noted that you may no longer need to use a trading broker. There are now many cryptocurrency wallets like Coinbase that will allow you to purchase cryptocurrencies directly from your cryptocurrency wallet account.

It bears stressing that you should not rush the process of choosing a cryptocurrency trading broker. It is very important that you get to work only with a trustworthy and reliable broker, so take as much time as you need to identify the right broker for you.

Chapter 12 The Future Of Cryptocurrency

You should now be well informed enough to start your investment in digital currencies and have a fair idea of what you are doing. As this market continues to grow and become more mainstream, the opportunities could be limitless. However, just with all new technologies, it could completely go bust in a few years like the big dot-com boom of the 90s. There is no way to predict where exactly this is headed. However you can be sure Blockchain and digital currencies will be around for a while, and more than likely they will become a major part of our daily lives in the near future.

So what is next for cryptocurrency? Cryptocurrencies continue to gain recognition and are being recognized as currency accepted by merchants, and this list is growing. But because this is such new technology, and to many people, such a complex idea, it may take a while for most of the population to accept it as a true form of money.

A recent survey puts millennials as the most likely to invest in cryptocurrencies. Many have said they would rather put money into Bitcoin than traditional stocks and bonds. Among those of the population ages 65 and up, there is only a small percentage who have even heard about cryptocurrencies, and less that would consider investing in them. This is a strong signal that Cryptocurrencies will remain a part of the future.

But millennial interest is not the only reason cryptocurrency is not going anywhere soon. New companies are joining the game every day, making 2018 projected to be one of the fiercest competitions yet for coin dominance. It is also expected that in 2018 more institutional investors will join the market, especially Bitcoin. This means that with each new company that embraces these digital currencies, they will slowly start to join the mainstream.

For a cryptocurrency to enter the mainstream financial industry, there are several things it will have to still overcome. Issues such as consumer protection, continue to allow anonymity but prevent tax evasion and money laundering. These are all pretty big issues to overcome. However, this all still remains in the to be determined categories of the digital currency world, the possibilities of one such currency eventually doing this, and breaking through to the mainstream financial world is still a possibility.

Because of this worldwide boom, many governments are starting to notice and get involved. Countries like Sweden, China, and Japan are working on creating their own government cryptocurrencies. This is expected to hit the markets within the next two years. It was recently released that the United State is also considering creating their own cryptocurrency.

The main lure of Bitcoin and cryptocurrencies, in general, was that there was no government involvement and that everything remained anonymous. However, with this massive boom and people making large amounts of money seemingly overnight, it was only time before Uncle Sam would come knocking.

Cryptocurrency and Taxes

The IRS has recently released a notice titled Notice 2014-21, which states that digital currency is to be treated as property. This means it can be used for federal tax purposes. And what that means is digital currency can be considered business property, personal property, or investment property. So basically taxpayers must track their currencies carefully so that a gain or loss can be recorded and reported to the IRS. You can do this by keeping each cryptocurrency in a separate wallet along with proper records. Because all records on the Blockchain are public, it should be easy to access and track these. Technology is being created to help taxpayers in this process.

So what is your decision now that you know all the basics needed to navigate the cryptocurrency world? Will you go long haul or take the risks and exchange currencies daily? The choice is yours, and hopefully, after reading this book, you can make some informed decisions.

Conclusion

As the world becomes more digitalized day by day, data security is one of the most burning issues. Cryptocurrencies are a considerable part of this change; therefore, it is vital for every user to be an expert in security measures.

Besides all those rules, there is one thing that could reduce the risk, and it is called "understatement". Even if you own Crypto assets over 1 million, you should never talk about it. Understatement can save you from robbery, hackers and false friends.

Finally, it is essential that indifferent which wallet you decide to use, always tell someone how to access your coins. Cryptocurrencies still have a considerable uncertainty ahead of them, and currently, most people do not know much about it. Therefore, even though this is something most people do not think about, you should always be aware of the possibility of dying or losing the ability to access your funds. It will be a significant loss if you have a considerable amount of assets, which your family cannot access because they do not know how. Take some time to create a "what if" plan. The positive side effect is that you might arouse the interest of your partner, children, parents or whomever.

www.ingramcontent.com/pod-product-compliance
Lightning Source LLC
Chambersburg PA
CBHW051452150726
48000CB00005B/2358